SCREAM
OF THE BUDDHA

SCOTT SHAW

Buddha Rose Publications

First Edition 1993
Second Edition 2011

ISBN: 1-877792-55-1
ISBN-13: 978-1-877792-55-7

10 9 8 7 6 5 4 3 2 1

Printed in the United States of America

SCREAM
OF THE BUDDHA

contents

6

I need the known love
that she has to offer me
in a world
that doesn't mean
anything at all

I need the known embrace
if only for a moment
to be held
in her arms

> a time
> to regain strength
> to go out
> and take on the world again

and the space
between the forms
is only paved in gold
gold and an ocean
air and mind and time

> what is the price
> I will pay it
> what is the cost
> it could never be too high
> for a moment
> another moment
> of her love
> Asian love
> in a western land
>
> I need to be held
> by her again

just slept this day off
it hurts too much
to think about it any-more

fade to a distant dream
that must be better
than zero reality

so somewhere/anywhere
but here

three

outside it calls me
tells me to go out

embraced by the darkness
held by the night
      and inside
      there is no dream
      only words
      spoken/written
      to the self
      but outside
      you never know
      what you will find

four

flip the stations
t.v. time/t.v. mind
a glass of the grape
    the clouds
    the fog
    I hear the ocean waves outside
    and I know
    I could go out of my mind

talking to myself
talking to a dream from the 1960s
1950s b&w screen
a moment of the 70s
as the 1990s are coming on
    time ticks
    I drink
    t.v. channels change
    and it all means the same
    nothing at all

and I speak
of willing
words of love
spoken to a woman
I do not even know
      like another late night
      black & white movie
      the air breathes
      its dark essence
          in the black
          of the night

I do not mean
a single word that I said to her
      life
      it has become
      such a lie

I do not mean it
I say it anyway
I wish I meant it
I wish I could remember
how to feel

      I look
      but there is nothing
      only the emptiness
      only the lie(s)

but
I made love with her
anyway

my coat
it lays on the floor
deep green
on light tan carpet
it lays next to my bed
black steel
black sheets
black blankets
        black
        it is the color of sinners

my robe
it lays on the floor
I threw it there
        evening last
took it off
while I made love to her
        her:
        black hair
        brown eyes
        small/Asian

I made love to her
I said goodbye
        goodbye
        until we meet another day
                another day – today

I told her
I would be at the airport
airport – LAX
        to join her
join her on her flight to Japan

I lied
I did not go
I hate myself for lying
I hate myself
for almost loving her
        I am the fool

her roommate
ex-roommate
she calls me tonight
the same day that her roommate
ex-roommate
left for home
left for Japan
she calls me
wants to make a date
for me
I have had her
have almost loved her too
        I say no

and it is all cast to the poetry
thrown into the nothing
written for other's eyes

        lived by one
        the two
        well, three of us
        actually

but what does it
what does life
mean, anyway...

she yells at me
across the courtyard
in *Farmer's Market*
with a Cajun accent

      funny, I guess
      I have had a lot of babes
      from Louisiana of late

she yells
she smiles
her rotting teeth show
surround by a face
      she is far too beautiful
      to have signs
      of such imperfection

we talk/we listen
we plan and dream of love
      physical
      as it may be

and in a passing moment
      destiny
      it is cast

      cast & lust
      lived & loved
      left only to this moment
      of a split second life
      in a secret woven place

eight

life ticks on
moments dream on
and the days
they do not mean
anything at all

    ten million things to do
    the world
    it works itself away

    a life w/ purpose
    a life w/ meaning
        bills to pay
        things to buy
    life it is here/it is gone

and what did it prove
and what could it mean

me, my biggest worry
is where will I eat lunch today

    hollow
    empty
    dance
    zero in a zero world

nine

I don't want to be alone tonight
but I'm tired
so tired
      tired of the nothing
      tired of the isolation
      tired of the hours
      that prove to be nothing
      tired of the confusion

I don't want to be alone tonight
but there is no one to call
I have rejected all the/my ladies
      for momentary macho
in a world that promises illusion
      around every turn

      and my mind it hurts
      from the forced insanity
      insanity in an insane world
         where do I turn
         who do I turn to

      and there is no one to save me

a babe
well, not exactly…
she sat down
at the table
to my right
    faces
    they surround me
    some
    I have seen before

    and she drinks iced tea
    w/ cream
    in the sunny and warm
    outdoor afternoon air

    and she gives me the glance
    with eyes of wanting

    today
    holds every chance
    every chance that ever was

    today
    it is everything
    that it could be
    it holds its all

    and today
    it is at hand
    and tomorrow
    I have no idea about

    so to her
    I say, *"Hello."*

eleven

I forgot
how to say I love you
in Korean
though there is no doubt that I do
       sweet child
       a decade younger than me
       innocence in your eyes
       in your walk/in your talk/in your mind

and maybe I am ten years too late
maybe you are ten years too early
maybe it just never was meant to be
       the holding hands
       the first kiss
       the love in my heart
       that I feel for you
       as I rob your innocence

perhaps it isn't the years
perhaps it is just destiny
       my being too tainted
       you being too young
       maybe, I don't know

but I wish I remembered
how to say I love you
in Korean
and I wish I had the keys
to the tickets of time

twelve

living
I don't
and the world dies

alone
time cries
addiction dies
and there is no place left to run

love
lost alone
who is left

nighttime
it grows old

a thought of you
I try to place your face in my mind
but I don't really remember
      your looks/your actions/your body
      though we spent last night together

I
who's space was much too altered
was it me
or was it you
      so unimposing
      so undefined
      as I stared at
      your ghost like Asian image
      nude
      through the shadows of the night
      last night

a thought
I want to remember
but I cannot recall
who you were

fourteen

20
31
years apart
but our touch
our lips
our bodies
they did meet

a decade ago
maybe I was just like her
young/trusting/ naïve

no
I was never
young/trusting/naïve

her words
they speak to me
her desires
lay upon me
like molasses
or peanut butter
        cold oil
        on a warm body

I would grab her
hold onto her forever
but all her embrace does
is to remind me of the years gone by
to no one else's eyes
and all the time wasted
chasing unhaveable dreams

I love you
but I kiss you goodbye
my sweet young child

the coffee doesn't make it tonight
is doesn't wake me up

a babe
across town
Chinese in *Little Tokyo*
    yeah, I am to meet her
    in an hour or so

but
will it all add up to so little
dollars/kisses/love
    tried and tasted
    known and felt all before

yeah, it doesn't mean anything
not anything at all

is it me
is it the world
is it the something
that always seems to equal
the nothing
I don't know

so I'll get into
my bad little *356*
cruise on over

I don't know
I guess I will live the depression
of passion
the promise
for a price

and maybe
just maybe
it will mean something
it will lead to something
maybe
something more
      than this nothing

maybe
I don't know

sixteen

sitting in the setting sun
no place left to be
kissing all the lonely nights
suicide is never free

and when
every place
turns into no place
when tomorrow
comes and then is gone
love
it proves its promise
it lies to us
because it never means anything
at all

she lays back onto me
smokes her cigarettes

the day
upon the ocean
closes in
as we sit upon my couch

yeah, we slept here
evening last
me
wrapped
in her Asian arms

and it almost meant something
something
in a world
that always holds the nothing
yeah, it was almost beautiful

a couch/my couch
this is where we spent the night
didn't even walk the ten steps to my bed
which waits in the other room
we just held each other
        tight
for a moment
        a night/a day
cast into nothing
        the couch
our developing love
holding each other tight
waking 1:00 o'clock
laying through the day

and nothing
it never has an ending
something
it does not know
where to begin
and love
is it for strangers
living in each other's arms

women who smoke
and days that dream
I hear Japanese
in my right ear
I hear the scream of the world
in my left
and what does it mean?
      nothing I suppose

outdoor
cool
winter's day
Farmer's Market
      it's Thursday, of course

red lipstick
and the smoke
blows from her lips
our eyes meet
a stare into the promise
a glace into the illusion
and the day is young
as I am becoming older
but you never know...

home at 4:00 AM
solo
I stick my head
beneath the covers
and I smell sex

a girl
well, make that two
no, make that three
this week
      the last five days
and I love them all
all three, differently
and so
when I told them
that I did
it was not a lie

home
alone
tonight
I prefer it that way

I stick my head
under the covers
and I smell sex

twenty

a dozen long-stemmed roses
Sunday
had to look the whole city over
to find them
but love
when it is at hand
it is always worth the cost
      bought & sold

so thank you
destiny
for the chance of meeting her
thank you god
for the only open flower shop
on Sunday
thank you
      my ex-babe
for taking me to the party
where I met my new love
      of a lover

dreams
      live hard
      die hard

twenty-one

roll over in the night
the dark
where the shadows
play havoc w/ your soul
I look
into her black eyes
I feel
her golden Asian body
     and for a moment
     I forget
     that this is something
     that may never happen again

     this moment to that
     my mind
     it wanders
     but I bring it back
     I hold her tight
     I kiss her neck
     for no matter how hard I try
     I know
     this moment
     can never be lived again

yeah, she told me all of her stories
she talks
words,
I have heard them all before
      that she is a good girl
      she's not like that...
      that she is old fashioned
      yeah, right

so we sip the wine – red
      expensive
      Italian
      old
then I walk with her
hand-in-hand
down the beach
      by where I live
she wants to sit down
she wants to kiss me
      and with a hand here
      a movement there
      my pup is planted
         another hoe goes down

so the stories
I have heard them all before
slapped hard
against the wall of the night
and yeah
they sound so good
but do I believe them?
fuck no

twenty-three

every night
I go to bed
w/ plans/dreams/things to do the next day
  try to make life better
  don't you know
then I wake up
and the naked form
of this Asian girl
a decade younger than me
  is next to my body
and they are all forgotten
  all the plans
I toss another day
to *never-never-land*
and just live the nothing of love

  would she
  would any babe
  do the same
  in my shoes

twenty-four

a drink
a woman
a drug
a journey
and then sometimes
        for a moment
I forget

twenty-five

I'm laying on the couch
a knock upon my door
      I get up
      I let her in
      I lay back down
      on the couch
      she lays down w/ me

      and for a moment
      in her embrace
      I am not alone

time
it is gone

I try to accomplish things
they equal nothing

should I try to accomplish no more

time
it is gone

I look into the mirror
age comes upon my face
  all the dreams
  all the hopes
  should I desire them no more

time it is gone

and what does it tell me
it says to me
that no matter what
we all die anyway…

twenty-seven

now my bro
Venchinzo and I
we party hard into the night
　　　most every night

a lot of clubs
a lot of bars
a lot of ladies
　　　drinkin' to do
　　　dancin' to do
　　　love makin' to do
and oh yes
we do wet our lips
with the nectar of the gods

most frequently
when we drink beer
then, it is all good
　　　we can drink
　　　all day/all night
　　　and come home
　　　none worse for the wear

　　　touch us
　　　with the harder elixirs
　　　and well...
　　　the equitation does change
　　　　　sometimes we get mighty
　　　　　fucked up

which brings me to this night
the one of which I speak...

now, I had met this girl
a sweet little Japanese number
introduced to me
by another one of my Japanese babes

"I'll wait for you forever."
she cried out to me
as I danced off with a new flavor

      so dancin' I did
      dancin' it was
      it was/she was
      what it/she was

      okay
      in the department of okay

the weird thing about her
she wore these glasses
      round
I thought she needed them to see
      see didn't
one day I took them off
tried them on
they were just glass
      she wore them for no good reason

her and I
we did what we did
as time ticked on
      she drank hard
      I liked that about her
      I like women who can drink

they are few
and far between

sex, with her
it was what it was
what it was
what it was
        just sex

anyway
to this night
the one of which I speak
she picks me up
        Redondo Beach
we pick up Venchinzo
        Venice
we drive to the head bangin' nightclub
of Tuesday night choice
        The Cathouse
        on Highland
        southern Hollywood

the tequila shot girl comes up
        her mistake
        hers
        or Venchinzo and mine
        I do not know
        we decide to pound hard
        I have my babe
        pick up the tab
                drink after drink
                shot after shot
                look out

"I'm out of money."
she/the babe
eventually claims
        no problem
        I start to pick up the tab

with no way to hit any new babe(s)
as I had one in tow
and fucked up
out of our minds
we hit out to the night
post one in the AM
just in time
to pick up a sixer at the local 711
over on Santa Monica B.L.V.D.

I climb into the backseat
of her white Japanese
eco-box sedan
we
Vencinizo and I
slam the brews
one after the other
        slam them fast and hard
        Budweiser
she drives

something strikes me strange
as we proceed down the freeway
        freedom
        this girl needs freedom

her expensive tennis racket
out the window
onto the freeway

"Stop! Don't do that!"

next, her leather jacket
        hits the payment
her books
her papers
        anything I can lay my hand on
        out the window

with nothing left to toss
I reach
her oh so precious
needed for nothing
plain glass
glasses
they go to the streets

finally
        without anything else
                her wallet
                her driver's license
                her purse
                they all hit the asphalt

Venchinzo
gets out
dropped off
        Venice

with nothing really to gain
nothing left to lose
    I decide
    tp pass out
she drives me home

she wake me up
as my door approaches
"You want to come in and make love?"
I inquire
she declined

     I go home
     I go to bed
     no better way
     to get rid of a girl
     you don't really want
     than to get rid
     of her everything

twenty-eight

I lay on the couch
sick as a dog
one too many
of the one too many
the night before

I lay here
watch the daytime reruns
try to forget how fucked I feel
I watch the reruns
of some ancient T.V. shows
from some years the previous
I try to forget
but they don't make me forget

I lay here
I hear the rumble
I began to feel the shake
      it continues/it lasts
my books
they go flying
from their shelves

my heart
goes into overdrive

my lamp
sways

my hanging guitar
swings

another fucking
L.A. earthquake

it just goes/flows
to its own rhythm
until it finds its time to stop

"Man. That it!"
"I am never going to do this again!"
    "Get drunk."
    "Get sick."
    "Never, not be full on again."
'cause you never know
what is going to come down

      the famous last words
      of every drunk

      never again
      until
      the next time

oh fuck,
I've got to go and throw up

twenty-nine

1990
I write it on a page
March
      damn, it is already
      that late in time/in my life

and the clock ticks on
and the days dream on
just counting the time
until death

and they tears they come
and the dreams they die
and what does it all
add up to, anyway?

another night
that means nothing at all

my ears ring
from the rock n' roll
still blasting in my soul
      nothing
        forever
          two words that equal
          the same thing

so I get her
pick her up
sleep with her
make love to her
      one more time

meaning-less time
a moment
to forget the emptiness
      the alone
      the life...

thirty-one

I stare across
a checked board
        yeah, a babe who like
        to play checkers

we sit on the floor
her and I

in the dimly lit recesses
of apartment house walls

her eyes
        soft
        Asian eyes
        they slant into the abyss

and I stare
into
the nothing that exists
w/ in them

a babe, yes
not alone, yes
a moment that means nothing, yes

but there has to be
something more to life

thirty-two

days
when you want to do something
but
you don't know what to do

thirty-three

when she sleeps
        she screams
when she makes love
        it is violent

and I love her

        the death
        the awaiting hand

        the sorrow
        the pain
        all waiting to come

        she knows it
        she leaves the door open
        a path for their arrival

        and there is nothing
        that I can do about it
                so I do nothing

        there is nothing
        nothing, nothing, nothing
        that needs/deserves
                a change

                so no change is made

thirty-four

my lady screams
    "I hate you!"
after I ask her
to do something for me

don't count the time(s)
that I stuck my neck out for her
don't count all of her bills I paid
that left me with all of my bill, unpaid
don't count all the things
which I missed out on
while I was doing things for her

my lady screams
    "I hate you!"

before it was all
so much more
      my giving
      equaled her taking
      her taking
      equaled my giving
turn it around
      one time
and the true nature of the beast
steps out

      I should have known better
        I guess...

as a tear
fights to come to my eyes
my lady screams
    "I hate you!"

night knocks hard
against the window
as I scream
for a reason to believe

thirty-six

I wake up humming
still hammered
from all the alcohol and coffee
I drank the night before

thirty-seven

I give another day to the nothing
write it off
to the zero
to the never-never-mean-nothing-land

thirty-eight

the first rays of sun
were gone
three hours ago
and me
I lay marked
like some drunken warrior
stabbed through the heart
with a knife
I lay
starring into the abyss
alone

54

thirty-nine

a bleeding/breathing afternoon
the zeros
     of the zero days
     long gone
as my cat
jumps up on
the couch
next to me
and I wonder why
I still write poetry
I wonder why
there is no longer
a moment of peace

I long for the days
where the cash was full-on
and I had a moment to dream

     in my fading youth
     in the afternoon
     cool breeze
     of the ocean wind

     time
     it always
     changes

sitting at *Farmer's Market*
my eyes caress the *L.A. Weekly*
for some reason
they are drawn to *The Personals*
     Asian female
     Looking for Romance
it said something like that...
I dropped her a line

a few days later
I get a response
we set a meet
down by her lo-cal
Newport Beach
Orange County
coffee house
Rock'n Java

there she was
this tiny-tiny-little girl
maybe four foot nothing
Hmong
     how bizarre

I told her I had once authored a book
on the *History of the Hmong*
she didn't believe me
didn't
until I knew more about her culture
than she

post/after
we hung/we fucked
I even drove up to Fresno

where she made her main crib
        a lot of Hmong's live up Fresno way
there we fucked too
her grandmother
        who she lived with
        told her she disrespected
        her people
        by hooking up with me
        at crib central
                that's probably true
                sorry grandma

        all pretty boring, right?
        yeah, that is what it was

she popped back to O.C.
a few weeks later
latched up at her cousin's crib
        or whomever it was
        she made residence with

she called me
I was set to hit the night
with Venchinzo
told her to come over
        "Bring a friend."
        she did
        she waltz into Venchinzo's
        tiny Venice apartment
        with a killer looking babe
        of the same breed
        even shorter than her
                my juices flowed

we were deciding where to go
as we did
I popped and killed a bottle of the grape
while Venchinzo
laughingly starred on
"That is pure poetry, man.
        They way you drink that stuff."
"I've had a lot of practice."

        funny
        Venchinzo
        Italian
        rarely
        drinks
        grape

with no clear destination
I call a friend of mine
who runs a club
up in Hollywood
as it is the current
all-cool-and-trendy-place
to be right now
        long lines, and all...
I call to make sure
the doorman
would be expecting me
        let us straight through the ropes

"Yeah, I got a couple of hoes in tow."
        so I told him
        on the telephone line

58

me and my big mouth
they didn't dig my words
they left

me, I said, *"Whatever."*
I'd been there/I'd done that

Venchinzo, however
        had not
he chases them out onto the street
        "He didn't mean anything by it!"
        "Come back!"

STRIKE ONE

They're gone
we hit a bar down the street from his place
a couple of fine
chocolate ladies were there
        we drink
        we talk
        we get fuck up
        we touch lips
                once/no twice

one had to call her kid
"I have to check on him."
Venchinzo speaks
*"He's probably just on the corner smokin'
crack."*

they bounce
didn't dig his words

STRIKE TWO

post a lot of drinkin'
we carry ourselves back to his place
we pass out

    somewhere through the night
    I woke up and puked on myself
        don't remember the incident

then
way too early in the AM
a knock comes upon Venchinzo's door
    this babe
    of his upstairs neighbor
        she looks at us
        she looks at him
        she looks at me
            covered in puke

"Why don't you loan him some clothes?"
"Why?"

STRIKE THREE

forty-one

so here I am
mid-thirty-two
sitting back
w/ a glass of the grape
sipping it
one too many times
refilling it
one more
for the road

yeah, one would think
that I would have
gotten over this by now
but the elixir promises passion
it promises release
from the pain

and the night
again...
the dream(s) die hard

     a woman called me
     I met her
     five days before
     I fell in love w/ her
          on the spot
     she called me
     asked me to call her
     she forgot to leave her number
     on my answering machine
     so I didn't/couldn't call her back

     my phone rings
     is it her?

her/now/again
has she called
when I am here to answer it
no
just some DM (dead meat)
of a done
one too many times
former babe/of a former flame

did her again and again and again
    as she spent my money
    god
    she spent a lot of my money
       now she's just a hoe

I hang up on her
    not interested

so I sit back
nowhere left to run
and drink another glass
of suicide

about the author

Scott Shaw is a prolific author, actor, artist, filmmaker, photographer, and composer. Shaw's poetry and literary fiction was first published by literary journals in the late 1970s. He continued forward to have several works of poetry and literary fiction published, in book form, during the 1980s. By the mid 1980s, after having spent years travelling extensively throughout Asia – documenting obscure aspects of Asian culture in words and on film, his writings on social science began to be published, as well. As the 1990s dawned, Shaw writings, based upon a lifelong involvement with the martial arts and eastern mysticism, began to be embraced. From this, he has authored literally hundreds of articles and a number of books on meditation, the martial arts, yoga, and Zen Buddhism; published by large publishing houses.

Scott Shaw's
books-in-print include:

About Peace: A 108 Ways to Be At Peace
        When Things Are Out of Control
Advanced Taekwondo
Bangkok and the Nights of Drunken Stupor
Bus Rides
Cambodian Refugees in Long Beach,
        California: The Definitive Study
Chi Kung For Beginners
China Deep
E.Q.
Essence: The Zen of Everything
Hapkido: Essays on Self-Defense
Hapkido: The Korean Art of Self Defense
Independent Filmmaking: Secrets of the Craft
Junk: The Backstreets of Bangkok
Last Will and Testament According to the
        Divine Rite of the Drug Cocaine
Marguerite Duras and Charles Bukowski:
        The Yin and Yang
        of Modern Erotic Literature
Mastering Health: The A to Z of Chi Kung
Nirvana in a Nutshell
No Kisses for the Sinner
On the Hard Edge of Hollywood
Sake' in a Glass, Sushi with Your Fingers:
        Fifteen Minutes in Tokyo
Scream: Southeast Asia and the Dream
Samurai Zen
Shanghai Whispers Shanghai Screams
Shattered Thoughts
Suicide Slowly
Taekwondo Basics

Ten to Thirty
The Ki Process:
      Korean Secrets for Cultivating
      Dynamic Energy
The Little Book of Yoga Breathing
The Little Book of Zen Mediation
The Lyrics
The Most Beautiful Woman in Shanghai
The Passionate Kiss of Illusion
The Screenplays
The Tao of Self Defense
The Warrior is Silent:
      Martial Arts and the Spiritual Path
TKO: A Lost Night in Tokyo
Yoga: The Spiritual Aspects
Zen Buddhism: The Pathway to Nirvana
Zen Filmmaking
Zen in the Blink of an Eye
Zen O'clock: Time to Be
Zen: Tales from the Journey